Table of Contents

Depression is one of the most common types of mental health conditions and often develops alongside anxiety.

Depression can be mild and short-lived or severe and long-lasting. Some people are affected by depression only once, while others may experience it multiple times.

Depression can lead to suicide, but this is preventable when appropriate support is provided. It's important to know that much can be done to help young people who are thinking about suicide.

Depression can happen as a reaction to something like abuse, violence in school, and the death of someone close or family problems like domestic violence or family breakdown. Someone might get depressed after being stressed for a long time. It can also run in the family. Sometimes we may not know why it happens.

BREAKFAST

1. Instant Pot Beef and Broccoli

Prep Time: 15 Minutes

Cook Time: 2hrs 2 Minutes

Servings: 4

Ingredients:

- 1 1/4 lbs. boneless beef chuck roast or flank steak sliced thinly across the grain
- 1/8 teaspoon sea salt and 1/4 teaspoon black pepper or to taste
- 1/2 teaspoon sesame oil
- 3 1/2 cups broccoli florets
- 1 tsp. xanthan gum OR arrowroot starch to thicken the sauce (leave out if desired)
- 1 tablespoon cold water

For The Sauce:

- 2 cloves garlic minced
- 1/2 teaspoon fresh minced or grated ginger

- 1/4 cup low sodium soy sauce use coconut amino for pale or Kato
- 1/2 cup beef broth
- 1/2 teaspoon erythritol or monk fruit sweetener (if not low carb you can add brown sugar)
- 1 teaspoon sesame oil
- 1/4 - 1/2 teaspoon red pepper chili flake or Sriracha optional

Instructions

For The Instant Pot Version:

1. Season beef with salt, pepper and 1/2 teaspoon sesame oil. Add 1-2 tablespoons of olive oil to the Instant Pot and press the SAUTE button. Once the Instant Pot is hot, sear the beef for 1-2 minutes until brown (cook in batches as needed).
2. In a medium bowl, whisk together all the ingredients for the sauce. Pour over beef.
3. PRESS Cancel, then press MANUAL or PRESSURE COOK on HIGH. Set to 4 minutes and cover with lid. Turn heating valve to SEAL.
4. Meanwhile, place broccoli in a microwave-safe bowl with 1/4 cup water. Microwave 2 – 3 minutes until

broccoli is tender. (Skip this step if you prefer and cook directly in the Instant Pot).

5. Quick release the pressure of the Instant Pot after the beef is cooked and there is a beeping to tell you it's done.

6. Carefully open the lid. To thicken the sauce, in a small bowl, whisk together xanthium or arrowroot starch with 1 tablespoon cold water. Whisk into the Instant Pot. Press SAUTE. (You can also transfer the beef to a bowl first if you prefer before whisking in the thickening slurry). Add the broccoli and cook until sauce has thickened and broccoli is hot.

7. Adjust seasonings and serve hot with your favorite sides - cauliflower rice or zoodles

For The Slow Cooker Version:

1. Season beef with salt, black pepper and 1/2 teaspoon sesame oil.

2. Combine all the ingredients for the sauce in the insert of a 5-6 quart slow cooker. Add the beef and toss to coat.

3. Cover and cook on HIGH for 45 minutes - 2 hours or LOW for 1.5 -3 hours (every slow cooker cooks at a different heating level - be sure to check times according to your slow cooker).

4. Meanwhile, place broccoli in a microwave-safe bowl with 1/4 cup water. Microwave 2 – 3 minutes until broccoli is tender (skip this step if you prefer and cook directly in the slow cooker).

5. Once the beef is done (or about 30 minute before serving) and if you prefer a thicker sauce, in a small bowl, whisk together xanthium or arrowroot starch with 1 tablespoon cold water. Whisk into the Slow Cooker (You can also transfer the beef to a bowl first if you prefer before whisking in the thickening slurry). Add the broccoli and cover and allow to cook on HIGH until sauce has thickened and or broccoli is tender (about 10-15 minutes).

6. Adjust seasonings and serve hot with your favorite sides - cauliflower rice or zoodles.

Prep Time: 12 Minutes

Cook Time: 8 Minutes

Servings: 4

Ingredients

For the lettuce wraps:

- 1 lb. boneless skinless chicken breasts or thighs cut into 1-inch cubes
- 1 teaspoon sesame oil
- Himalayan salt and black pepper to taste
- 2-3 tablespoons olive oil
- 1 medium red bell pepper seeded and diced
- 1 cup broccoli florets chopped
- 1 head butter or romaine lettuce leaves separated and rinsed
- Roasted cashews optional
- Thinly sliced green onions for serving, optional
- Sesame seeds for serving, optional

For The Sauce:

- 1/3 cup coconut amino low sodium soy sauce gluten free tamari or low-sodium soy sauce
- 1 tablespoon rice wine or apple cider vinegar
- 1/2 teaspoon low carb sweetener xylitol optional, for sweetness
- 2 teaspoon sesame oil
- 2 medium cloves garlic minced
- 1 teaspoon grated fresh ginger
- 1-2 teaspoons arrowroot starch to thicken - optional

Almond Butter Sauce:

- 1/4 cup creamy almond butter
- 1 teaspoon sesame oil
- 1 teaspoon rice wine or apple cider vinegar

Instructions

1. Season chicken with salt, black pepper and 1 teaspoon sesame oil. Set aside.
2. Heat a large wok or skillet over medium-high heat. Add 1 1/2 tablespoons olive oil and saute chicken until cooked through, about 4-5 minutes. Transfer to a plate.

3. Return pan to heat and add remaining olive oil. Add the bell peppers and broccoli and stir-fry for 3-4 minutes, or until tender crisp.

4. Meanwhile, whisk together the ingredients for the sauce and stir into pan along with the cooked chicken.

5. Divide among lettuce wraps and top with cashews, sesame seeds and green onions, if desired.

Prep Time: 15 Minutes

Cook Time: 1hr 3 Minutes

Servings: 16

Ingredients

For the crust:

- 1/3 cup ghee or refined coconut oil softened
- 3 tbsp. yacon syrup OR Lecanto Sugar-free maple syrup, or preferred liquid sweetener
- 1 tsp. vanilla
- 2 cups superfine almond flour
- 3 tbsp. coconut flour

For the filling:

- 15 oz. can pumpkin puree not pumpkin pie filling
- 1/2 cup canned coconut cream or use the thick part of full-fat canned coconut milk
- 3 tbsp. Lecanto Sugar-free maple syrup or preferred liquid sweetener
- 1/4 cup golden monk fruit sweetener or preferred brown sugar substitute

- 1 tsp. vanilla extract
- 1/4 tsp. fine grain sea salt
- 2 1/2 tsp. pumpkin pie spice
- 1/2 tsp. ground cinnamon
- 2 large eggs room temperature

For the Topping:

- Coconut whipped cream
- Pumpkin pie spice

Instructions

1. Preheat the oven to 350°F and line an 8×8 pan with parchment paper, leaving a slight overhang. Set aside.
2. In a large bowl, combine the coconut oil, sugar-free maple syrup and vanilla until smooth. Sift in the almond flour and coconut flour and mix until the dough forms and comes together.
3. Press the dough into the bottom of the lined pan and bake for 11-13 minutes, or until golden. Remove from the oven and allow to cool slightly.
4. In a large bowl, beat the eggs, then whisk in the pumpkin puree, coconut cream, sweeteners, vanilla, pumpkin pie spice and cinnamon and mix until well

combined and smooth. Alternatively, blend the ingredients in a food processor or blender until smooth.

5. Bake: Pour the filling over the crust and tap gently on the counter to remove any air bubbles. Bake for 50-60 minutes, or until its set and the filling no longer jiggles.

6. Let Cool & Chill: Remove your bars from the oven and allow them to cool completely at room temperature before covering them with plastic wrap and transferring them to the fridge for 6-8 hours, or overnight.

7. Cut, Add Topping & Serve: Once cool, cut into 12 even bars and top each bar with piped whipped cream or a dollop of coconut cream sprinkled with a little bit of pumpkin pie spice.

Prep Time: 15 Minutes

Cook Time: 25 Minutes

Servings: 6

Ingredients:

- 1/4 cup solid refined organic coconut oil OR solid ghee you want the texture to be similar to softened room temperature butter
- 3 tablespoons creamy unsalted cashew butter OR pecan butter (can also sub with creamy unsalted nut butter or seed butter of choice but cashew butter OR pecan butter gives the best flavor profile)
- 1/4 cup Lecanto sugar-free maple syrup OR pure maple syrup for paleo
- 1/2 tablespoon vanilla extract
- 1 1/2 cups superfine blanched almond flour
- 3 tablespoons coconut flour sifted
- 1/2 teaspoon baking soda
- ½ teaspoon cream of tartar
- 1/8 teaspoon fine sea salt
- 1/2 teaspoon cinnamon

- For the cinnamon sugar topping
- ¼ cup golden monk fruit sweetener OR coconut sugar for paleo
- 1 tablespoon cinnamon

Instructions

1. Line a large baking sheet with parchment paper and set aside.

2. MIX THE WET INGREDIENTS: In a large mixing bowl, whisk together the nut butter, softened coconut oil, maple syrup and vanilla until smooth.

3. Top view of paleo pumpkin bread batter in a white bowl with a wooden spoon

Prep Time: 10 Minutes

Cook Time: 25 Minutes

Servings: 4

Ingredients:

- 8-10 chicken tenders or 6 chicken thighs
- Salt and black pepper to taste
- 3 tablespoons low sodium soy sauce OR coconut amino
- 3 tablespoons fresh lemon juice 1 lemon
- 2 tablespoons unsalted butter. Melted
- 1/2 tablespoon finely chopped cilantro can leave out if you're not a fan of cilantro

Seasonings:

- 1 1/2 teaspoons salt
- 1/2 teaspoon garlic powder
- ½ teaspoon black pepper
- 1/2 teaspoon chili powder leave out if sensitive to spice
- 1/2 teaspoon cumin
- 1/2 teaspoon smoked paprika

For the vegetables:

- 1 cup broccoli florets
- 1 lb. bunch of asparagus trimmed

For meal prepping:

- Side of your choice: cauliflower rice or zoodles
- 4-5 lunch containers

Instructions

1. Preheat oven to 400°F. Spray a large sturdy baking sheet with cooking spray or for easier clean-up, line with parchment paper or heavy duty foil.
2. Place the chicken on prepared baking sheet. Season with salt and black pepper to taste.
3. In a small bowl, combine soy sauce, lemon juice, butter and cilantro together. Drizzle 1/3 of the sauce over the chicken.
4. Bake for 5 minutes (20 for chicken thighs). Meanwhile, combine the seasonings in a small bowl and set aside.
5. After 5 minutes, remove baking pan from the oven, flip the chicken and place the asparagus and broccoli along the sides of the chicken. Sprinkle the chicken and vegetables with seasonings and drizzle sauce over the

vegetables and some more on the chicken (reserve 1 teaspoon for the end).

6. Return the oven back to the pan and bake for another 10-15 minutes, or once the chicken is cooked through and has reached an internal temperature of 165°F. (You may want to remove the vegetables first (so they don't overcook) if the chicken is not cooked through yet, depending on your level of preference.)

7. Drizzle the chicken with additional sauce and turn the oven to broil for -2 minutes, until the chicken has a nice brown color (watch closely so the chicken does not burn).

8. Sprinkle with chopped parsley, if desired and serve hot.

Prep Time: 5 Minutes

Cook Time: 10 Minutes

Servings: 4

Ingredients:

- 2 large eggs
- 4 tablespoons canned organic pumpkin OR pure pumpkin puree NOT pumpkin pie filling
- 2 tablespoons cashew butter, almond butter OR nut or seed butter of your choice
- 2 tablespoons monk fruit sweetener, you can add more if you prefer sweeter pancakes
- 2 tablespoons unsweetened almond milk
- 1/2 teaspoon pure vanilla extract
- 2/3 cup super-fine blanched almond flour
- 2 tablespoons coconut flour
- 1 teaspoon baking powder
- 1 teaspoon pumpkin pie spice
- 1/2 teaspoon ground cinnamon
- Cooking spray or ghee for griddle

Optional For Extra Fluffy Pancakes:

- 1 egg white whipped to stiff peaks

Instructions

1. In a large bowl, beat the eggs then whisk in the pumpkin, nut or seed butter and monk fruit sweetener. Pour in the milk and vanilla and mix until smooth.]
2. Add almond flour, coconut flour, pumpkin pie spice, cinnamon, salt, and baking powder and stir until the batter is combined. The batter should be somewhat thick.

(Optional Step For Thicker & Fluffier Pancakes: Whip up an egg white until stiff peaks form. Gently old into the pancake batter.

1. Allow the batter to rest for 3-5 minutes.
2. Preheat griddle or a large skillet on medium-low heat - medium heat. It's important to allow the pancakes to cook low and slow since they are grain free.
3. Coat griddle or pan with avocado or coconut oil cooking spray or ghee.
4. Drop scant 1/4 cup rounds onto the griddle. Cook until the edges begin to turn golden brown and bubbles form

on the top, about 3-5 minutes. GENTLY flip and cook another 2-4 minutes or until golden brown and the middle is cooked through.

5. Serve or top with desired toppings: sugar free syrup, chopped nuts, almond butter, melted ghee/ butter or whipped coconut cream, if desired.

Prep Time: 10 Minutes

Cook Time: 27 Minutes

Servings: 16

Ingredients:

- 3/4 cup chopped dark chocolate unsweetened, divided
- 1/4 cup unsalted butter
- 1/4 cup coconut oil
- 2 tablespoons natural almond butter creamy / unsalted
- 1/2 cup powdered erythritol
- 2 teaspoons pure vanilla extract
- 1/8 teaspoon fine sea salt
- 2 large eggs room temperature
- 1/2 cup unsweetened cocoa powder
- 1/2 cup finely ground blanched almond flour
- Pinch of sea salt for topping (optional)

Instructions

1. Preheat oven to 325 F. Line an 8x8 square pan with parchment paper leaving a slight overhang (for easier removal). Set aside.

2. In a large heat-safe bowl, heat 1/2 cup of the chopped chocolate, almond butter and coconut oil over a double-boiler on the stove or in the microwave in 20-second increments, until chocolate is just melted and smooth (stir well in between - do not overheat).

3. Whisk in sweeteners, vanilla and salt. Add the eggs one by one and whisk until incorporated. Stir in cocoa powder followed by the almond flour until just combined (do not over mix). Fold in remaining 1/4 cup chopped chocolate. The batter will be thick.

4. Spread batter into prepared pan and smooth with an offset spatula.

5. Bake in preheated oven for 23-27 minutes - under bake for fudgier brownies. Allow to completely cool before slicing into even squares.

6. Top with pinch of sea salt, if desired.

Prep Time: 15 Minutes

Cook Time: 1hr 3 Minutes

Servings: 16

Ingredients:

For the crust:

- 1/3 cup ghee or refined coconut oil softened
- 3 tbsp. yacon syrup OR Lecanto Sugar-free maple syrup, or preferred liquid sweetener
- 1 tsp. vanilla
- 2 cups superfine almond flour
- 3 tbsp. coconut flour
- For the Filling
- 15 oz. can pumpkin puree not pumpkin pie filling
- 1/2 cup canned coconut cream or use the thick part of full-fat canned coconut milk
- 3 tbsp. Lecanto Sugar-free maple syrup or preferred liquid sweetener
- 1/4 cup golden monk fruit sweetener or preferred brown sugar substitute

- 1 tsp. vanilla extract
- 1/4 tsp. fine grain sea salt
- 2 1/2 tsp. pumpkin pie spice
- 1/2 tsp. ground cinnamon
- 2 large eggs room temperature

For the Topping:

- Coconut whipped cream
- Pumpkin pie spice

Instructions

1. Preheat the oven to 350°F and line an 8×8 pan with parchment paper, leaving a slight overhang. Set aside.
2. In a large bowl, combine the coconut oil, sugar-free maple syrup and vanilla until smooth. Sift in the almond flour and coconut flour and mix until the dough forms and comes together.
3. Press the dough into the bottom of the lined pan and bake for 11-13 minutes, or until golden. Remove from the oven and allow to cool slightly.
4. In a large bowl, beat the eggs, then whisk in the pumpkin puree, coconut cream, sweeteners, vanilla, pumpkin pie spice and cinnamon and mix until well

combined and smooth. Alternatively, blend the ingredients in a food processor or blender until smooth.

5. Bake: Pour the filling over the crust and tap gently on the counter to remove any air bubbles. Bake for 50-60 minutes, or until it's set and the filling no longer jiggles.

6. Let Cool & Chill: Remove your bars from the oven and allow them to cool completely at room temperature before covering them with plastic wrap and transferring them to the fridge for 6-8 hours, or overnight.

7. Cut, Add Topping & Serve: Once cool, cut into 12 even bars and top each bar with piped whipped cream or a dollop of coconut cream sprinkled with a little bit of pumpkin pie spice.

Prep Time: 10 Minutes

Cook Time: 17 Minutes

Servings: 12

Ingredients:

- 3 large eggs room temperature
- 1/4 cup drippy almond butter
- 1/4 cup coconut oil melted and cooled
- 3 tablespoons almond milk
- 1 cup canned pumpkin or pure pumpkin puree - NOT pumpkin pie filling
- 3/4 cup golden monk fruit sweetener OR coconut sugar for paleo
- 1 1/2 teaspoons pure vanilla extract
- 1 1/3 cups superfine blanched almond flour
- 1 tablespoon pumpkin pie spice
- 1 teaspoon baking powder
- 3/4 teaspoon baking soda

Optional Add-Ins:

- 1/3 cup sugar free chocolate chips (we used Lily's) plus more for topping if desired
- 1 1/2 Tablespoon chopped pecans

Instructions

1. PREP MUFFIN PAN AND PREHEAT OVEN: Preheat the oven to 375°F. Grease or line a 12 pan muffin tin with parchment paper liners and grease with coconut oil (it's important to grease them otherwise they will stick to the liners).
2. MIX THE WET INGREDIENTS: In a large bowl, beat the eggs until fluffy then add the pumpkin puree, nut butter, low carb sweetener, coconut oil, milk and vanilla. Mix well until fully combined.
3. ADD THE DRY INGREDIENTS: Stir in the almond flour, pumpkin pie spice, baking powder and baking soda and mix until combined. Fold in the chocolate chips and nuts, if using.
4. DIVIDE BATTER: Divide the batter evenly between the prepared muffin tins (I use a large cookie scoop) and top with extra chocolate chips or pecans if desired.

5. BAKE: Bake in preheated oven for 17-19 minutes or until a toothpick inserted into the center of a muffin comes out clean.

6. Remove pan from oven and allow the muffins to cool in pan for 10 minutes

Prep Time: 10 Minutes

Cook Time: 30 Minutes

Servings: 4

Ingredients

- 1 tablespoon olive oil or butter
- 1/4 onion, diced
- 1/2 pound asparagus, tough ends trimmed and cut into 2" pieces
- 1/3 cup chopped broccoli florets
- 1/2 red bell pepper chopped
- 2 pieces deli-ham (preferably nitrate free), chopped (we like Applegate)
- Himalayan pink salt and black pepper to taste
- 8 large eggs
- 1/4 cup heavy cream OR coconut cream (can also sub with unsweetened almond milk)
- 1/2 teaspoon garlic powder
- 1/2 cup grated cheddar cheese
- 4 ounces goat cheese
- Salt and pepper

Instructions

1. Preheat oven to 400 F degrees with the rack in the middle position.

2. In a 10″ nonstick skillet over medium heat, heat the oil or butter and add the onions, asparagus, broccoli and bell peppers. Cook for 2-3 minutes, until just becoming tender. Stir in chopped ham. Season with a pinch of salt and pepper.

3. Meanwhile, whisk the eggs with cream and season with additional salt and pepper. Stir in the garlic powder, ham and cheddar cheese. Pour the eggs into the same pan with the asparagus, and top with crumbled goat cheese.

4. Transfer the pan to the oven and cook until the the frittata is just set, about 15-18 minutes.

5. Cut into wedges and serve warm.

11. Keto Pumpkin Bread

Prep Time: 10 Minutes

Cook Time: 50 Minutes

Servings: 12

Ingredients:

- 3 large eggs room temperature
- 1 cup canned pumpkin or pure pumpkin puree - NOT pumpkin pie filling
- 1/3 cup drippy almond butter
- 1/4 cup coconut oil melted and cooled
- 1/4 cup almond milk
- 2/3 cup golden monk fruit sweetener OR coconut sugar for paleo
- 1 1/2 teaspoons pure vanilla extract
- 1 1/2 cups superfine blanched almond flour
- 1 tablespoon coconut flour
- 1 tablespoon pumpkin pie spice
- 1 teaspoon baking powder
- 3/4 teaspoon baking soda

Optional Add-Ins

- 1/3 cup sugar free chocolate chips (we used Lily's) plus more for topping if desired
- 1 1/2 Tablespoon chopped pecans

Instructions

1. PREP LOAF PAN AND PREHEAT OVEN: Preheat The Oven To 350ºf. Grease A 9"X5" Loaf Pan, And Line with Parchment Paper.
2. MIX THE WET INGREDIENTS: In a large bowl, beat the eggs until fluffy then add the pumpkin puree, nut butter, low carb sweetener, coconut oil, milk and vanilla. Mix well until fully combined.
3. ADD THE DRY INGREDIENTS: Stir in the almond flour, coconut flour, pumpkin pie spice, baking powder and baking soda and mix until combined. Fold in the chocolate chips and nuts, if using.
4. TRANSFER BATTER TO PAN: Pour the batter into the prepared loaf pan.
5. BAKE: Bake in preheated oven for 44 - 52 minutes, or until a toothpick inserted into the center of the loaf comes out clean

6. Remove pan from oven and loaf to cool in pan for 10
   minutes.

Prep Time: 10 Minutes

Cook Time: 15 Minutes

Servings: 1

Ingredients:

- 1/3 lb. ground turkey
- 1/2 teaspoon avocado oil
- 2 teaspoons garlic powder
- Salt and black pepper to taste
- 2 cups green leaf lettuce butter lettuce or greens of choice
- 2 strips cooked crispy bacon roughly chopped
- 1/4 cup sliced cucumbers
- 3 sliced pickles
- 1/2 avocado sliced
- 2 cherry tomatoes cut into halves
- 1 tablespoon red onion chopped
- OPTIONAL: leave out for Whole30 and Paleo
- 1-2 tablespoons shredded cheese

Optional Sauce:

- 2 tablespoons Whole30 compliant avocado oil mayonnaise we use Primal Kitchen
- 1 tablespoons Whole30 compliant ketchup we used Primal Kitchen
- 1 teaspoon coconut amino

Instructions

1. In a large skillet, heat avocado oil over medium heat, add ground meat and season with garlic powder, salt and pepper. Cook until brown, while crumbling and drain any excess grease.
2. Assemble bowl starting with greens then add browned meat and arrange remaining toppings around meat.
3. Mix the ingredients together for the sauce, top over burger bowl and serve.

Prep Time: 10 Minutes

Cook Time: 10 Minutes

Servings: 4

Ingredients:

- 2 teaspoons avocado oil
- 3 green onions sliced, green & white parts divided
- 3 cloves garlic, minced
- 1 teaspoon ginger, freshly grated or minced
- 1 lb ground turkey, or ground pork, chicken or beef
- Salt and black pepper, to taste
- 3 tablespoons coconut amino, if not Whole30 can also use tamari or low sodium soy sauce
- 2 teaspoon fish sauce, can also use 1/2 teaspoon Trader Joe's Mushroom Umami Seasoning if preferred
- 2 teaspoons apple cider vinegar, or rice vinegar
- 1/2 teaspoon toasted sesame oil
- 6 cups shredded green cabbage, or one 10 oz. tri-color coleslaw mix or Broccoli Slaw
- 1 cup shredded purple cabbage, leave out if using coleslaw mix

- 1/4 cup grated carrots, leave out if using coleslaw mix

For serving:

- Sesame seeds
- Fresh chopped parsley
- Your favorite compliant chili sauce sriracha, Gochujang, etc.

Instructions

1. Heat avocado oil in a wok or large skillet over medium heat. Add the white parts of the green onion, garlic and ginger and cook for 1 minute until fragrant.
2. Next, add the ground turkey, while breaking it up and cook until browned and cooked through.
3. Add the shredded cabbage (or coleslaw mix) followed by the carrots, coconut amino, fish sauce, sesame oil, vinegar and season with salt and black pepper as needed. Toss until the vegetables are tender-crisp (about 3 minutes). Taste and add additional coconut amino, salt, black pepper as needed.
4. Garnish with cilantro, green onions and sesame seeds.
5. Serve over cauliflower rice with chili sauce, along with any of your favorite sides.

Prep Time: 15 Minutes

Cook Time: 10 Minutes

Servings: 4

Ingredients:

- 1/2 - 1 lb extra-lean ground turkey omit if you want to keep this a meatless dish
- 1/2 cup mushrooms sliced
- 2-3 cloves of garlic minced
- 1/2 tablespoon olive oil
- 5-6 Medium Zucchini peeled
- 1 14.5-ounce can diced tomatoes (I recommend San Marzano or fire-roasted tomatoes)
- 1 8-ounce can tomato sauce
- 3 tablespoons tomato paste
- 1 1/2 teaspoons dried oregano
- 1/2 teaspoon crushed red pepper flakes optional
- Salt and ground black pepper to taste
- 2 1/2 tablespoons of fresh chopped basil divided
- 2 tablespoons chopped fresh parsley leaves
- 1 cup part-skim mozzarella cheese shredded

- 2/3 cup fat-free cottage cheese
- 1/3 cup low-fat ricotta cheese for garnish optional
- Sprinkle of parmesan cheese for garnish optional
- Optional add-ins
- 1 1/2 - 2 cups spinach chopped
- 2 medium zucchini peeled and chopped
- 1/4 cup water reserved as needed

Instructions

1. Prepare the zucchini noodles:
2. Paralyze zucchini using the ribbon blade or a vegetable peeler; set aside. Pat dry with a paper towel. (This step can be done up to 3 days in advance. Simply store zoodles in an airtight container with a paper towel to help absorb excess moisture.)
3. Heat the olive oil in a large skillet over medium-high heat, add in the ground meat and cook until browned, about 3-4 minutes, making sure to crumble and break down into small pieces as it cooks; drain excess fat.
4. Add the garlic and saute for 30 seconds to a minute or until fragrant. Add mushrooms and optional chopped zucchini, if using and saute for 4 minutes. Season with salt and pepper to taste. Add tomato paste, diced

tomatoes, tomato sauce, oregano, red pepper flakes and 1 tablespoon of basil. Bring to a boil and reduce heat allowing to simmer. Stir constantly until sauce begins to thicken (about 5 minutes).

5. Add the rib boned zucchini noodles and cover with lid.

6. After 2 minutes, remove cover, swirl the zucchini around using tongs to avoid sticking to the pan.

7. Continue cooking until zucchini is tender (another 2-5 minutes). If adding spinach, stir in after 3 minutes and cover.

8. Remove from heat and stir in mozzarella and cottage cheese. Taste and adjust seasonings as needed.

9. Top with dollops of ricotta cheese. Cover with pan and allow to sit for 2-3 minutes or until the cheese has melted.

10. Add water as needed if the sauce is evaporating.

Prep Time: 5 Minutes

Cook Time: 20 Minutes

Servings: 9

Ingredients:

- 6- 9 large eggs
- 1 cup water
- Instant Pot steamer rack
- Instant Pot

Instructions

For The Instant Pot Method:

1. Insert the steam rack in the inner pot of the Instant Pot. Pour water inside.
2. Place the eggs on top of the steam rack that comes with the Instant Pot
3. Close and seal the lid. Move valve to sealing. .
4. Press The Manual Or Pressure Cook (High) Button And Adjust Time To:

5. For Soft Boiled Eggs For A Runny - Partially Cooked Yolk: 2-3 Minutes

6. For Soft Boiled Eggs With An Almost Cooked Yolk: 4 Minutes

7. For Hard Boiled Eggs: 5 Minutes

8. Allow 5-10 minutes for the Instant Pot to come to pressure. After the selected minutes are up and the eggs are cooked:

9. Immediately do a quick release by using a long spoon and push the valve to venting - allow all the steam to release. Carefully unlock and open the lid.

10. Quickly transfer eggs to a large bowl with ice cold water and keep running water until cool enough to hold. Allow eggs to sit in very cold water until completely cool. When the eggs are cool, gently crack and peel.

For The Stove-Top Method:

1. Place the eggs in a medium-large (depending on how many you make) pot and cover with cold water.

2. Cover with lid and set the pot over high heat and bring the water to a rolling boil

3. As soon as the water comes to a boil, immediately remove the pot from the heat and allow to sit, covered for the correct time depending on desired doneness below:

4. For hard boiled eggs:

5. 15 minutes

6. For soft boiled eggs:

7. 4-6 minutes

8. Quickly transfer eggs to a large bowl with ice cold water and keep running water until cool enough to hold. Allow eggs to sit in very cold water until completely cool. When the eggs are cool, gently crack and peel.

Prep Time: 12 Minutes

Cook Time: 15 Minutes

Servings: 4

Ingredients

For the fajita seasoning:

- 2 teaspoons chili powder
- 1 teaspoons cumin
- 1 teaspoon garlic powder
- 1 teaspoon onion powder
- 1 teaspoon smoked paprika
- 1/2 teaspoon salt or to taste
- 1/4 teaspoon black pepper or to taste

For the fajitas:

- 3 tablespoons olive oil divided
- 1/4 cup fresh cilantro leaves chopped plus more for serving
- Juice from 2 limes divided
- 1 tablespoon Dijon mustard paleo/Kato brand as necessary OR Worcestershire sauce

- 1½ pounds skirt or flank steak halved crosswise
- 4 medium bell peppers seeded and thinly sliced I used red, yellow, orange and green
- 1 medium red onion thinly sliced
- 1-2 tablespoons unsalted butter

For serving:

- Lime wedges
- Sliced avocado
- Low carb tortillas or cauliflower rice for serving

For Meal Prep:

Lunch containers

- 1 - 1 1/2 pounds medium white shrimp peeled and deveined
- 4 medium bell peppers seeded and thinly sliced I used red, yellow, orange and green
- 1 medium red onion thinly sliced
- 3 tablespoons unsalted butter melted OR olive oil
- juice from 2 limes divided

Seasonings:

- 2 teaspoons chili powder
- 1 teaspoons cumin

- 1 teaspoon garlic powder
- 1 teaspoons smoked paprika
- 1/2 teaspoon salt or to taste
- 1/4 teaspoon black pepper or to taste
- chopped fresh cilantro for serving
- lime wedges for serving
- sliced avocado for serving
- coconut wraps cauliflower rice or zoodles for serving
- For Meal Prep: Lunch Containers

Instructions

1. Combine all the ingredients for the fajita seasonings. Reserve 1 1/2 teaspoons for the bell peppers.
2. In a medium bowl, combine 2 tablespoons of olive oil, chopped cilantro, lime juice, mustard and 5 teaspoons of the fajita seasonings. Reserve 1 tablespoon of the steak marinade for drizzling on the steak at the end. Pour remainder of the steak marinade into a large zip-top bag along with the steak. Press the bag to evenly distribute the marinade and allow to sit while you prepare the vegetables.
3. Slice the the onions and bell peppers.

4. Heat 1 tablespoon olive oil in a 12" skillet over medium high heat. Add the onions and allow to cook for about 5 minutes, or until softened and fragrant. Add the bell peppers and sprinkle with the reserved 1 1/2 teaspoons of fajita seasonings. If you like the peppers with a nice crunch - cook for about 3-5 minutes. And if you like them softer, leave them on for about 3 minutes longer. Transfer and set aside on a plate.

5. Melt butter on the same skillet and sear the steak. Allow to sear for 3 to 4 minutes (or more depending on how done you like your steak) on each side. Transfer steak to a cutting board and allow to rest for at least 5 minutes before slicing into thin strips. Add the reserved steak marinade to the skillet and add the steak strips until just heated. Remove from heat.

6. Serve hot with warm tortillas, avocado slices and lime wedges.

Prep Time: 8 Minutes

Cook Time: 12 Minutes

Servings: 4

Ingredients:

- 1 - 1 1/2 pounds medium white shrimp peeled and deveined
- 4 medium bell peppers seeded and thinly sliced I used red, yellow, orange and green
- 1 medium red onion thinly sliced
- 3 tablespoons unsalted butter melted OR olive oil
- Juice from 2 limes divided

Seasonings

- 2 teaspoons chili powder
- 1 teaspoons cumin
- 1 teaspoon garlic powder
- 1 teaspoons smoked paprika
- 1/2 teaspoon salt or to taste
- 1/4 teaspoon black pepper or to taste
- Chopped fresh cilantro for serving

- Lime wedges for serving

- Sliced avocado for serving

- Coconut wraps cauliflower rice or zoodles for serving

Instructions

1. Preheat oven to 425 degrees. Line with parchment paper or foil for easier clean cup.

2. In a large bowl, combine the shrimp, peppers and onions together. Drizzle with melted butter and juice from 1 lime. Add chili powder, cumin, garlic powder, paprika, salt and pepper. Toss everything well to coat with seasonings.

3. Spread the shrimp and vegetables in an even layer on prepared sheet pan. Try not to overlap too much and keep everything in a single layer.

4. Bake in preheated oven for 8-13 minutes until peppers are tender and shrimp is cooked through and no longer pink. Broil on high for 2 minutes so the shrimp gets that nice char (optional).

5. Drizzle with additional lime juice and chopped cilantro, if desired. Serve in heated tortillas with sliced avocado and your favorite toppings.

6. Serve in coconut wraps, over salad or cauliflower rice.

Prep Time: 20 Minutes

Cook Time: 20 Minutes

Servings: 2

Ingredients

- 1-2 boneless skinless chicken breasts, pounded to even thickness
- Salt and black pepper to taste
- 1 tablespoon olive oil
- 2 avocados peeled pitted and cut into slices (or chopped)
- 4 cups chopped mixed green lettuce
- 3 hard-boiled eggs peeled and sliced
- 6 slices bacon cooked and chopped
- 1 cup grape or cherry tomatoes halved
- ½ cucumber sliced in rounds or chopped
- ½ cup crumbled feta or blue cheese

For the vinaigrette:

- 3-4 tablespoons apple cider vinegar
- 2 tablespoons sour cream

- ½ teaspoon garlic powder
- 2 tablespoons extra virgin olive oil
- Salt and pepper to taste
- In a reseal able zip-top bag add chicken, salt, pepper, balsamic vinegar and garlic and marinate for at least 30 minutes.

Instructions

1. In a reseal able zip-top bag, add chicken, salt, pepper, balsamic vinegar and garlic and marinate for at least 30 minutes.
2. To make the hard boiled eggs:
3. Place the eggs in a medium pot and fill with enough water to cover the eggs.
4. Cover with lid and set the pot over high heat and bring the water to a rolling boil
5. As soon as the water comes to a boil, immediately remove the pot from the heat and allow to sit, covered for 15 minutes. Using tongs, transfer eggs to a large bowl with ice cold water and keep running the cold water into the bowl until the water stays cool (or alternatively place in an ice bath). Allow eggs to sit in the chilled water until completely cool (I leave mine for

about 8-10 minutes). Once the eggs are cool, crack, peel and slice.

Grill the chicken:

1. Preheat grill to medium-high heat and cook for 4-5 minutes on each side or until the internal temperature reaches 165 F. Remove the chicken from the grill and tent with foil. Let it rest and cool a bit for about 10 minutes and then slice or chop into bite-sized pieces.

Assemble the salad:

2. Whisk together all the ingredients for the vinaigrette. Drizzle 1 teaspoon over the sliced avocado (to prevent from browning).
3. In a large bowl, add the lettuce, then top with cooked pasta, eggs, avocado, bacon, tomatoes, cucumber and cheese. Drizzle with dressing right before serving.

Prep Time: 5 Minutes

Cook Time: 3 Minutes

Servings: 4

Ingredients:

- 1 lb raw medium shrimp peeled, de-veined and tails removed
- Salt and black pepper to taste
- 1 tablespoon chipotle peppers in adobo sauce, finely minced
- 1/2 tsp. chili powder
- 1/4 tsp. cumin
- ¼ tsp. garlic powder
- ¼ tsp. onion powder
- 1/4 tsp. smoked paprika
- Zest and juice of 1 lime
- 2-3 bell peppers thinly sliced
- 1 onion thinly sliced
- 1 tablespoon avocado or olive oil divided
- 1 tablespoon butter

To serve:

- Cauliflower rice
- Fresh cilantro
- Lime wedges
- Avocado slices or guacamole

Instructions

1. In a medium bowl, combine shrimp, salt, black pepper, chipotle peppers, chili powder, cumin, garlic powder, onion powder, paprika and lime. Set aside.
2. Slice the onions and peppers.
3. Heat 1 tablespoon oil and cook peppers and onions 4-5 minutes, stirring regularly, or until they're crisp-tender. Transfer to plate. Wipe down the pan as necessary.
4. Heat butter and remaining oil in same skillet over medium heat. Working in batches, sear shrimp and cook for 2-3 minutes per side. Transfer to plate, and continue cooking remaining shrimp, adding more oil and /or butter as necessary. When all the shrimp is cooked add everything including the peppers back to the pan and tossing very gently until heated through. Add a splash of lime and adjust seasonings.

5. Serve over cooked cauliflower rice with cilantro, lime wedges and avocado, if desired.

Prep Time: 15 Minutes

Cook Time: 10 Minutes

Servings: 4

Ingredients

- 3/4 - 1 pound ground turkey
- 1/2 teaspoon Himalayan salt plus more to taste
- 1/4 teaspoon black pepper
- 1/2 cup red bell pepper finely diced
- 1 tablespoon sliced olives
- 3 tablespoons tomato sauce
- 3/4 teaspoon taco seasoning
- 1/2 cup shredded Colby Jack or cheddar cheese plus more for topping
- 2-3 medium Haas avocados cut in half and pits removed
- 2-3 tablespoons shredded cabbage red & green
- 2 tablespoons fresh chopped cilantro

Instructions

1. In a large skillet, add turkey and brown until cooked through. Drain any grease then season with salt and black pepper.

2. Add bell pepper, olives, tomato sauce, taco seasoning and stir to evenly combine ingredients. Allow to cook for 2-3 minutes, until heated through. Taste and adjust seasonings. Remove skillet from heat and stir in shredded cheese.

3. Fill each avocado half with 2-3 tablespoons of the turkey mixture. Sprinkle with cabbage, fresh cilantro, additional cheese and serve.

21. Chili Lime Chicken Lettuce Wraps

Prep Time: 15 Minutes

Cook Time: 12 Minutes

Servings: 4

Ingredients

For the fajita seasoning:

- 2 teaspoons chili powder
- 1 teaspoons cumin
- 1 teaspoon garlic powder
- 1 teaspoon onion powder
- 1 teaspoon smoked paprika
- 1/2 teaspoon salt or to taste
- 1/4 teaspoon black pepper or to taste

For the fajitas:

- 3 tablespoons olive oil
- 1/4 cup fresh cilantro leaves chopped plus more for serving
- Juice from 2 limes divided

- 1 1/2 pounds chicken thighs sliced
- 4 medium bell peppers seeded and thinly sliced I used red yellow orange and green
- 1 medium red onion thinly sliced
- 1 head butter lettuce leaves washed green leaf or romaine works too
- Sliced avocado and lime wedges for serving

Instructions

1. Combine all the ingredients for the fajita seasonings. Reserve 1 1/2 teaspoons for the bell peppers.
2. In a medium bowl, combine 1 tablespoon of olive oil, chopped cilantro, lime juice and 3-4 teaspoons of the fajita seasonings. Reserve 2 tablespoons of the chicken marinade for drizzling on the chicken at the end.
3. Pour remainder of the marinade into a large zip-top bag along with the chicken. Seal bag tightly and press the bag with your hands to evenly distribute the marinade and allow to sit while you prepare the vegetables.
4. Slice the onions and bell peppers.
5. Heat 1 tablespoon olive oil (or butter for Kato) in a 12" skillet over medium high heat. Add the onions and

allow to cook for about 5 minutes, or until softened and fragrant. Add the bell peppers and sprinkle with 1 - 1 1/2 teaspoons of the reserved fajita seasonings. If you like the peppers with a nice crunch - cook for about 3-5 minutes. And if you like them softer, leave them on for about 3 minutes longer. Transfer and set aside on a plate.

6. Melt remaining 1 tablespoon of oil on the same skillet and brown the chicken. Cook for 5-6 minutes, or until cooked through. Add the reserved chicken marinade to the skillet and cook for an additional 30 seconds. Remove from heat.

7. Assemble lettuce wraps by placing a spoonful of chicken/vegetable filling into the center of each leaf. Top with avocado or your favorite toppings.

Prep Time: 10 Minutes

Cook Time: 15 Minutes

Servings: 2

Ingredients:

- 8 hard-boiled eggs roughly chopped
- 2 ripe medium avocados
- 2 tablespoons mayonnaise
- 1-2 tablespoons Dijon mustard to taste
- Juice of 1/2 lemon
- Sea salt to taste
- Freshly cracked black pepper to taste
- 1/2 - 1 tablespoon fresh dill chopped to taste

Optional serving suggestions:

- Lettuce wraps
- Low carb wraps
- Kale and cabbage slaw

Instructions

Cook the eggs:

1. Cover the eggs with very hot tap water in a saucepan. Bring to a boil, turn heat off, cover with lid and remove from heat. Allow to sit for 18 minutes. Uncover and pour out hot water. Run under very cold water and allow to sit for 5-10 minutes until cool. Peel and chop.

2. In a large bowl, mash the avocados using a fork. Add the chopped eggs, yogurt, mustard and lemon juice and mix to combine. Season with salt, black pepper and dill, to taste.

3. Serve immediately at room temperature, or chill and serve cold.

4. Serving suggestions: Enjoy alone, spread between two slices of bread with kale & cabbage slaw for an Avocado Egg Salad Sandwich, add to pita or scoop into lettuce wraps for a low carb Kato version.

Prep Time: 10 Minutes

Cook Time: 15 Minutes

Servings: 12

Ingredients:

- 9 Different Flavor Options
- Base (Classic) Recipe - Start Here For All Of The Flavors
- 12 large eggs
- Himalayan sea salt and freshly ground pepper to taste
- Optional toppings:
- Shredded cheese dried oregano dried basil, freshly chopped parsley
- For The Bacon Egg Cup - 12 Cooked Bacon Strips
- For The Cauliflower And Cheese Egg Cup - 1 Cup Cauliflower Rice & 1 Cup Shredded Cheese
- For The Salami Egg Cup - 24 Genoa Salami Slices
- For The Ham & Cheddar Egg Cup - 12 Thin Deli Ham Slices
- For The Proscuitto Egg Cup - 12 Thin Prosciutto Slices

- For The Sweet Potato Egg Cup - 24 Shaved Sweet Potato Ribbons (Use A Mandolin Or A Vegetable Peeler) (Skip This Flavor For Low Carb)
- For The Turnip Egg Cup - 24- Shaved Turnip Ribbons
- For The Zucchini Egg Cup - 24 Shaved Zucchini Ribbons (Use A Mandolin Or A Vegetable Peeler)

Instructions

1. Preheat oven to 375°F and grease or line a 12 cup muffin pan with silicone muffin liners.

Base Recipe:

2. Line the bottom and sides of each muffin tin with meat or veggie slices of your choice - feel free to mix and match or make all the egg cups the same.

For Over-Easy Eggs:

3. Crack an egg into each muffin tin. Season with salt and pepper. Add optional toppings.
4. Bake for 12-15 minutes or until eggs are firm. Remove and serve hot.

For Omelette Styled Baked Eggs:

1. Crack the eggs in large measuring cup (feel free to swap out some whole egg with egg whites, if preferred). Season with salt, pepper and herbs of your choice. Pour mixture into muffin cups, dividing evenly amongst each cup.

2. Bake for 12-15 minutes or until eggs are firm. Remove and serve hot.

Prep Time: 12 Minutes

Cook Time: 15 Minutes

Servings: 4

Ingredients:

For the homemade taco seasoning:

- 2 teaspoons chili powder
- 1 teaspoon cumin
- 1 teaspoon sea salt
- 1/4 teaspoon black pepper
- 1/2 teaspoon garlic powder
- 1/2 teaspoon onion powder
- 1/4 teaspoon oregano
- 1/4 teaspoon paprika

For the meat:

- 1 lb ground beef or turkey
- 2 tablespoon tomato paste
- 2 teaspoons apple cider vinegar

For the taco bowls:

- Cauliflower rice (or use your favorite cooked rice or quinoa
- 1 small zucchini sliced into thin halves
- 1-2 bell pepper chopped (any color works)
- 1/2 cup shredded cabbage green & red
- 1/2 cup grape tomatoes
- Olive slices
- Avocado slices
- Lime wedges

Other optional taco toppings:

- Shredded lettuce shredded cheese, Pico de Gallo, salsa, guacamole etc.

Instructions

1. In a small bowl or small reseal able spice jar, combine all the spices for the taco seasoning. You can save any leftovers for the next time.
2. In a large nonstick skillet, over medium high heat, cook the ground meat, breaking down into small pieces while it cooks. After about 3 minutes, add 1 tablespoon of the taco seasoning and continue cooking until the meat is no longer pink and cooked through. Stir in the

tomato paste and vinegar and cook for another 2 minutes or until everything is heated through. Taste and add more seasoning as needed.

Prep Time: 8Minutes

Cook Time: 15Minutes

Servings: 4

Ingredients

- 4 medium chicken breasts pounded to even thickness OR 6-8 boneless chicken thighs skinless or with skin
- Sea salt and pepper to taste
- 1/2 teaspoon garlic powder
- 1/2 teaspoon red chili flakes optional or to taste
- 3 tablespoons butter swap with olive oil for paleo
- 1/2 small onion chopped
- 4 garlic cloves sliced or minced
- 2 teaspoons Italian seasoning
- 1/2 teaspoon lemon zest
- Juice of 1 medium lemon
- 3-4 tablespoons heavy cream leave out for paleo
- Chopped fresh parsley and lemon slices optional for garnish
- Cast Iron Skillet

Instructions

1. Season chicken with salt, pepper and garlic powder. Heat olive oil in a medium-sized cast iron skillet over medium-high heat. Add chicken and cook for 4-5 minutes on each side, or until chicken reaches 165 degrees. Transfer browned chicken to plate and set aside.

2. Return pan back to heat and melt butter. Stir in the onions and garlic. Add lemon juice to deglaze pan and cook for 1 minute. Add Italian seasoning, lemon zest and chicken broth. Stir in heavy cream and allow to thicken and bubble. Add the chicken back into the pan until heated through.

3. Sprinkle chicken with chopped parsley and serve hot with your favorite sides. Spoon sauce over chicken and garnish with lemon slices, if desired.

Prep Time: 10 Minutes

Cook Time: 20 Minutes

Servings: 6

Ingredients:

- 6-8 boneless chicken thighs skinless or with skin
- Sea salt and pepper to taste
- 1/2 teaspoon garlic powder
- 1/2 teaspoon dried thyme
- 1/2 teaspoon dried rosemary
- 2 tablespoons olive oil
- 3 tablespoons ghee swap with butter if not paleo
- 2 tablespoons chopped onion
- 2 garlic cloves sliced or minced
- 1 1/2 tablespoons balsamic vinegar
- 1/2 cup homemade or low sodium chicken broth
- 2 cups Brussels sprouts, about 1/2 pound, trimmed and halved
- 1 cup chopped pumpkin, or butternut squash if not low carb
- 1 cup broccoli florets

- 1 small yellow zucchini, quartered
- Chopped fresh parsley or thyme
- Instant Pot I have the 6 Quart Instant Pot DUO
- OR Cast Iron Skillet

Instructions

1. Season the chicken with salt, pepper, garlic powder, thyme, rosemary and sage.
2. To cook in the Instant Pot:
3. Press the Sauté function (Normal setting) on the Instant Pot and add the olive oil to the pot. (I use a 6 Quart Instant Pot DUO)
4. Place chicken in the Instant Pot and cook on each side for 2-3 minutes, or until golden brown. This helps to seal in the juices and keep it tender. (You may have to work in batches depending on the size and amount of chicken you are using). Once browned, remove from Instant Pot and set aside.
5. Melt ghee in the Instant Pot and stir in the onions and garlic. Add balsamic vinegar to deglaze pan and cook for 1 minute.
6. Add the chicken broth along with the browned chicken back into the Instant Pot. Add the pumpkin and

Brussels sprouts. Lock the lid, and turn the valve to SEALING.

7. Select the Manual (older models) or Pressure Cook (newer models) button and adjust the timer to 7 minutes.

8. It will take about 5-10 minutes to come to pressure and start counting down.

9. When done, do a quick release, then remove your Instant Pot lid. Add the broccoli and zucchini then close the lid for 2 minutes to steam.

10. Once the broccoli is tender, remove chicken and all the vegetables to a platter; cover loosely to keep warm.

11. Press saute and cook any remaining sauce for about 2-3 minutes until slightly thickened.

12. Serve sauce with chicken and vegetables; sprinkle with rosemary and parsley, if desired.

Prep Time: 12 Minutes

Cook Time: 15 Minutes

Servings: 4

Ingredients

Olive oil for the grill

- 10-12 raw large shrimp deveined, tails on or off
- Salt & pepper to taste
- 1/2 teaspoon Italian seasoning
- 1/4 teaspoon smoked paprika, optional
- 4 cups baby spinach
- 1 -2 cups green leaf or romaine lettuce, chopped
- 1 cup cherry tomatoes
- 2 medium avocados, diced
- 1/4 cup chopped pecans
- 1/4 cup sliced almonds
- 1/2 tablespoon feta crumbled, optional - leave out for Paleo & Whole 30

For the Dressing:

- 1/3 cup extra virgin olive oil

- 2 tablespoons apple cider vinegar
- 1 1/2 tablespoon compliant Dijon mustard
- 2 teaspoons fresh lemon juice
- 1 1/2 teaspoons poppy seeds
- Salt and black pepper to taste

Instructions

1. Preheat the grill (or grill pan) to medium-high. Using a brush, clean the grill and grease with oil using a long pair of tongs with some folded paper towels dipped in some olive oil.
2. Season your shrimp with salt, black pepper, Italian seasoning and paprika.
3. To make the dressing:
4. Combine the olive oil, vinegar, mustard, lemon juice, poppy seeds, salt and pepper in a jar or a bowl and mix well until all ingredients are incorporated and set aside.
5. Grill shrimp for 3-4 minutes on each side or until shrimp is opaque.
6. To assemble the salad:
7. Add the spinach or mixed greens to large bowl. Add 1/3 of the dressing and toss to combine.

8. Add the avocado, tomatoes, pecans and almonds.

9. Pour the remainder of the dressing over salad and toss to combine. Divide salad among 2-4 bowls.

10. Top each salad bowl with some cooked shrimp and feta (if desired) and serve immediately.

Prep Time: 15 Minutes

Cook Time: 10 Minutes

Servings: 4

Ingredients

For the Wasabi Cream:

- 3 tablespoons mayonnaise
- 1 tablespoon water
- 2 teaspoons wasabi paste

For the sushi bowls:

- 16 ounces riced cauliflower about 4 cups fresh or frozen
- 2 tablespoons water
- 1 tablespoon coconut oil
- 1 tablespoon toasted sesame oil
- 8 ounces lump crabmeat I used canned
- 2 tablespoons mayonnaise
- 2 teaspoons Sriracha sauce
- 1/2 avocado sliced
- 1 sheet nor seaweed cut into thick strips
- 1/2 medium cucumber cut into matchsticks or rounds

- 1/3 cup shredded red cabbage for garnish
- 1/2 medium radish sliced into thin rounds for garnish
- 1 teaspoon grated carrots for garnish optional

Instructions

To make the wasabi cream:

1. Mix the ingredients for the cream in a small bowl until well combined.

For the sushi bowls:

2. In a medium saucepan over medium heat, combine the cauliflower with the water and coconut oil Bring to a simmer, then cover and reduce the heat to low. Cook for 5 to 10 minutes, until tender. Remove from the heat and let cool completely. Stir in the sesame oil.

3. In a medium bowl, combine the crab meat, mayonnaise and Sriracha. Stir until well mixed.

4. Divide the cauliflower rice among 4 serving bowls. Top each with one-quarter o the crab mixture, avocado slices, noni strips, cucumber, and shredded cabbage and radish slices, if desired. Sprinkle with sesame seeds. Serve with the wasabi cream on the side.

Prep Time: 15 Minutes

Cook Time: 7 Minutes

Servings: 4

Ingredients

Olive oil for the grill

- 1 lb about 24 raw jumbo shrimp peeled and deveined tails on
- Himalayan Pink salt and ground pepper to taste
- 2 1/2 teaspoons chopped fresh oregano or 1 teaspoon dried oregano
- 2 1/2 teaspoons chopped fresh thyme or 3/4 teaspoon dried thyme
- 1 1/2 tablespoons finely minced garlic
- 1 tablespoon chopped fresh parsley plus more for serving, if desired
- Metal or wooden skewers
- 2 tablespoons fresh lemon juice

Instructions

1. Preheat the grill (or grill pan) to medium-high. Using a brush, clean the grill and grease with oil using a long pair of tongs with some folded paper towels dipped in some olive oil.

2. Season the shrimp with salt, pepper, garlic, oregano, and 2 teaspoons parsley in a medium bowl. Toss to combine.

3. Thread the shrimp onto skewers. If using wooden skewers, soak them in water for 30 minutes ahead of time to prevent burning and splintering.

4. In a small bowl, combine the melted ghee (or butter), garlic, lemon juice and another 1 teaspoon parsley together. Brush lemon butter sauce on both sides of shrimp, reserving some for later.

5. Grill skewers for 3-4 minutes on each side or until shrimp is opaque and vegetables are tender or starting to brown just slightly.

6. Brush remaining lemon sauce over the shrimp and allow to cook for 10 more seconds.

7. Remove from heat and serve with some more fresh herbs and lemon wedges, if desired.

Prep Time: 15 Minutes

Cook Time: 12 Minutes

Servings: 4

Ingredients

Heavy Duty Foil plus parchment paper if preferred

Seasonings:

- 2 teaspoons chili powder
- 1 teaspoon cumin
- 1 teaspoon garlic powder
- 1 teaspoons smoked paprika
- 1/2 - 1 teaspoon sea salt or to taste
- 1/4 - 1/2 teaspoon freshly ground black pepper or to taste
- 1/8 teaspoon cayenne pepper optional or to taste

For the foil packets

- 12 ounces flank steak sliced into 1/4" strips across the grain
- 3 tablespoons olive oil divided

- Juice from 2 limes divided
- 1/2 teaspoon Worcestershire sauce
- 2-3 medium bell peppers
- 1 medium red onion thinly sliced

For serving:

- Chopped fresh cilantro
- Lime wedges
- Sliced avocado
- Warm tortillas flour or corn
- For Low Carb: Low Carb Tortillas Or Cauliflower Rice, For Serving

Instructions

1. Preheat grill to medium-high heat or the oven to 425 degrees F.
2. Combine the ingredients for the seasonings in small bowl or bag and mix.
3. In a large bowl, add the steak and drizzle with 1 1/2 tablespoons olive oil, juice from 1 lime and Worcestershire sauce. Sprinkle with 2/3 of the seasonings. Toss to coat well. (If time permits, allow to

marinate at least 30 minutes or covered in fridge for up to 3 hours for maximum flavor).

4. Cut four 18 x 12 inch squares of foil and lay out on a flat surface.

5. Place the steak in the middle of each piece of foil.

6. Cut the veggies into thin strips and drizzle with olive oil and the remaining 1/3 of the seasoning mix. Divide evenly into each packet, arranging them around the steak.

7. Fold the foil over the steak and seal to close off the packets.

9 798395 550965